Tube Bandit

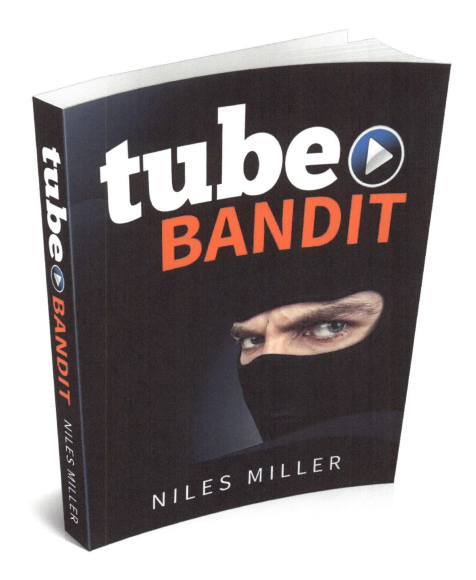

Table of Contents

One of the easiest and fastest ways to make money online quickly is to promote affiliate products on Clickbank or Warrior Plus using Youtube.

Just make a short Youtube video reviewing any product. For Clickbank, look for products above $30 with a commision of at least 50% and a gravity over 20.

It is best to look for products with gravity between 30-100. Products with gravity over 100 have tons of competition. So, it is much easier to go after the products in the sweet spot.

The gravity is the number of affiliates that have made a sale. The ones that have worked best for me are health related problems like acne, moles, anxiety, warts, etc.

You don't have to appear on camera to make these videos, you can just record the screen if you like. They only need to be 1-2 minutes long.

You can use Google Hangouts to make these videos, so you don't have to worry about buying expensive screen recording software.

All you need to do is add your affiliate link below the video and or in annotations.

This is the basic outline of course. The key is to get the videos up so the commision with start to roll in fast. Don't worry about making them perfect.

The first step is to go to click bank.com and sign up for an account if you don't have one. It is simple and free to sign up and search the marketplace for something that you would like to promote.

This can be anything that interests you. For me, I seem to have the best luck with health related problems.

For example: I sold quite a few acne e-books.
Make sure that the product sells for at least $30 with the commission of at least 50%.

This way you will make a decent commission. I try for a minimum of $15, but $20 and up is the sweet spot.

For me, the cheaper products did not sell any better anyway, so why waste your time doing the same amount of work. Also, make sure the gravity is 20 or above.

The gravity is a number of affiliates that have made at least one sale. This way you know others are making sales. So, it is a proven seller.

You can sort the list at the top by popularity, gravity, etc.

just pick five products that meet the above criteria form [Clickbank.com](). You can promote any offers such as Warrior plus, CPA, etc. There are unlimited possibilities.

Just take something that seems to be in demand and looks good to you. Would you buy this product?

The next step is to set up a Youtube account/channel if you don't have one. This is very easy. Here is a good current [step by step video]() if you need help.

This will only take a few minutes and allow you to promote multiply products.It is a good idea to set up niche related channel.

Example: Weightloss channel-You can promote several weight loss, fitness, nutriction, etc. just make sure there are plenty of products to promote. You don't want to take an obscure niche with few products.
I know several people that have done very well creating channels about their hobbies. As I mentioned this is only good if there is plenty to promote in your niche.

Make sure you get your account verified. You need a phone number for this. I have used a landline and just picked up and I also had other accounts verified with a text sent to my cell.

You are only allowed 2 accounts verified per phone number. So, make sure there is plenty of products to promote in your niche. You can also get a free google voice phone number if you need more accounts verified.

Setting up Google Hangouts. This is nice because you do not have to have screen recording software like Camtasia. Also, Google hangouts ranks extremely well.

You will need a Google account. If you don't have one, just sign up for Gmail. This is very easy and will only take about 1-2 mins.

You can use your real name or a pen name. You can also pick and e-mail related to your niche.

After you set up a Google account, login and head over to Google hangouts to get started creating your video.

To get started, click the g+.

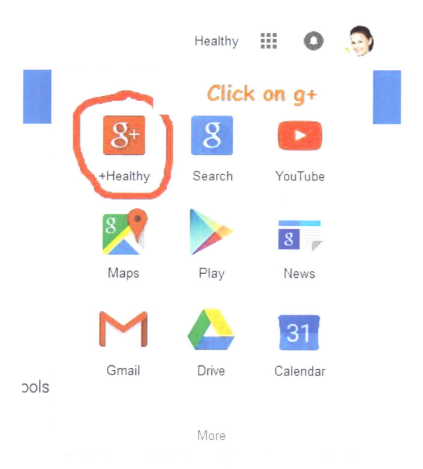

Next, click on the Hangouts with the green quotes.

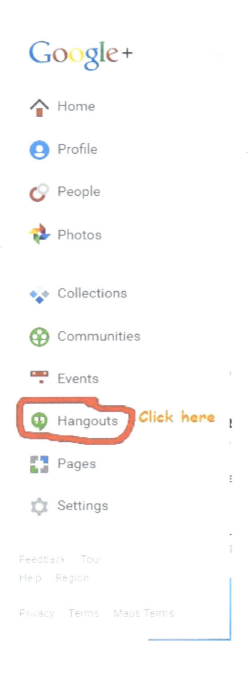

Google+

↑ Home

👤 Profile

People

Photos

Collections

Communities

Events

Hangouts   *Click here*

Pages

⚙ Settings

Feedback Tour
Help Region

Privacy Terms Maps Terms

Next, click the Hangouts on Air text.

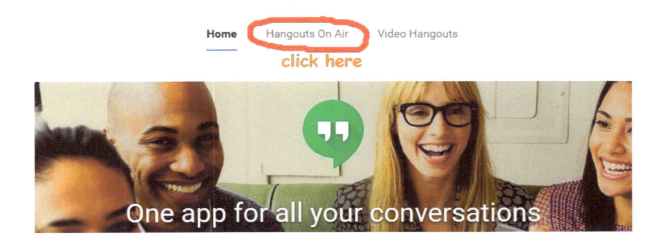

Next, click the yellow Create a Hangout on Air button.

Fill and the title and description then click the green share button.

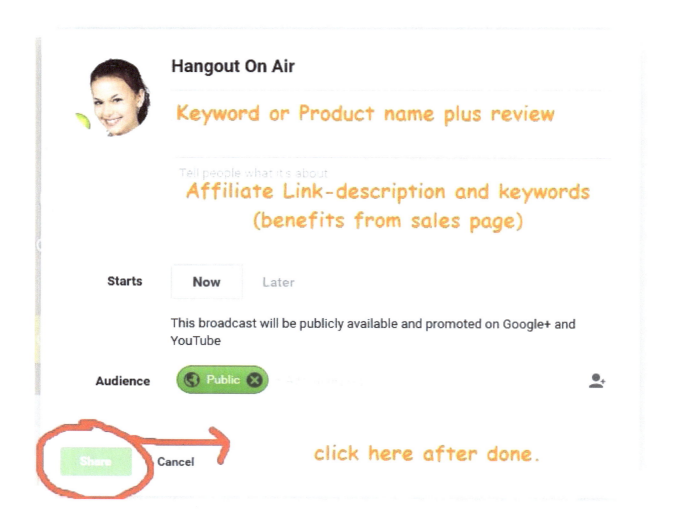

Pick the keywords for the title. You can use the product name plus review. Go to utube and look at the most popular videos with the most views like yours to get some keyword ideas.

Don't copy their title, but you can use something similar. Also, check Google search and planner for more ideas.

Then brainstorm to come up with some ideas for keywords. As soon as you type in the first keyword, Google will give you several suggestions.

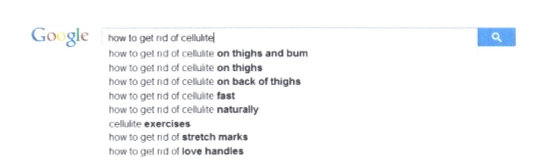

Also, type in the product name and review of the product. Example-Acne Away review.

Don't spend too long on this. You will never make any commision until you get some videos up.

I have put reviews up really quickly that have made sales right away. So, don't worry about being perfect.

If the views are in the millions, this is probably someone with a lot of subscribers and follows so the views could be misleading.

Therefore, look at several videos to get the best keywords. It is also good to check Google and Google planner for more ideas.

You are now ready to begin recording, click the blue start button.

 test 1

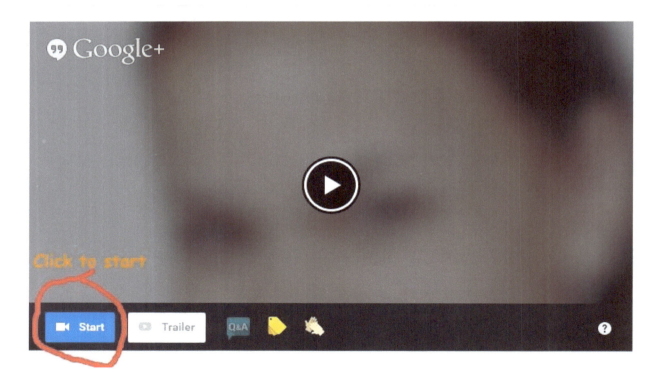

Skip the invite guests by clicking the white skip button.

Invite guests

+ Add names, circles, or email addresses

Your YouTube account is connected to your Google+ page or profile
This Hangout On Air will be broadcast on Google+ (by Healthy Living1) and on
your YouTube account (Healthy Living1).

☐ Require guests to be 18+ to join this video call

Invite   Skip   Click here

This is the showcase. To get to this click on left upper column and select the yellow tags. It is the third app down. Type in the actual raw affiliate link. Cloaked links are not allowed here.

Delete the profiles and fill in your raw affiliate link. No cloaked links are allowed here.

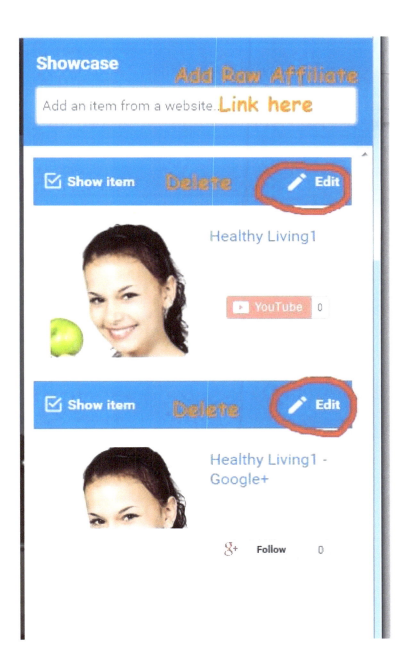

Click the green Start Broadcast button to begin recording your review video. Make this between 1-3 minutes long and tell them to click the link below the video.

It is set up by default to show you talking on camera. If you don't want this you can turn the camera off or hit screen share (the second icon down on the left menu-green box with an arrow)

This will allow you to share the screen. You can do a preview of the product and review. Click the blue OK button to get your video started.

Just record your review. Just talk a little about the problem it solves and then give some benefits of the product. You can find these by reading through the product or sales page.

Of course, it is best to buy or get a review copy of the product if possible.

Videos with tips seem to do very well on YouTube. Example: 3 Natural Ways to Get Rid of Acne in 5 Days!

Just add your link below the Video and tell them to click on the link below the video to get more tips.

The video only needs to be 1-2 minutes. If you feel uncomfortable, hire someone on Fiverr for $5 to do it.

After you are done recording, click the red stop broadcast button.

The video will be automatically sent to your Youtube channel in about 5 minutes or so. This makes things really easy!

Next, just click the blue close button.

This Hangout On Air is now over

A recording of the broadcast will now be uploaded to your YouTube channel and will automatically replace the live video players that were shared. Please allow a few minutes for the upload and processing to complete. You will be able to view the recording in your YouTube Video Manager.

Close

To improve your video ranking, you can add backlinks for free here http://pingomatic.com/

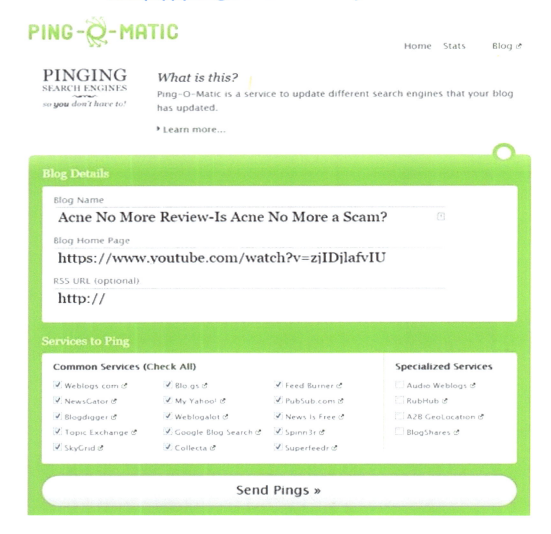

If you want to really crank up the backlinks, head over to Fiverr and purchase a backlinking gig.

Here is a super ninja trick that I just learned. Purchase more than one Fiverr gig to add extra backlinks.

But, make sure they are from different providers, so the links come from different sources. This will help you greatly improve your ranking.

The key to making this system work, is to get the videos up. You don't always need a zillion views to make sales. I have done reviews that made sales in as little as 5 views, so you never know who will bite.

It reminds me of fishing. The first time you cast your bait into the water you could get a bite.

The people that I have seen do the best are the ones that offered free tips and have a Youtube "Niche" channel.

Examples: (weight loss, fishing, beauty, healthy eating, cooking, etc) This could be anything. However, it is probably best to make sure there are products to promote in your niche.

A lot of people create a Youtube channel for their hobby. This is awesome! Just make sure there are some things to promote.

Good luck and start getting some review and tip videos up on your Youtube channel so you can start collecting some cash!

You need to take action and cast your bait so you can start getting some bites.

Thank you,
 Niles Miller.
http://
onlineshoppingden.com